YOUR CASE

for

LOVE

HOW TO GIVE IT AND HOW TO GET IT

14 Lessons to Understand How To Make True Connection

Inspired by the historic time of COVID-19 and Black Lives Matter

TONY DEE

Published by Composition Matters, LLC
1765 E. Nine Mile Road Suite 1, #221
Pensacola, Florida 32514

Disclaimer Notice:

Please note the information contained within this document is for educational and entertainment purposes only. All effort has been executed to present accurate, up to date, reliable, complete information. No warranties of any kind are declared or implied.

Readers acknowledge that the author is not engaging in the rendering of legal, financial, medical or professional advice. The content within this book has been derived from his life and various sources.

By reading this document, the reader agrees that under no circumstances is the author responsible for any losses, direct or indirect, that are incurred as a result of the use of information contained within this document, including, but not limited to, errors, omissions, or inaccuracy

Note from the Author

Here's the thing: doctors know the human body is complex. It is so complex that different practices have been developed to address each part of the body. Love is as complex as the body that hosts it. Here are several reasons.

Love affects the mind and the body. I'm not just talking about sex. If your love life is out of alignment, your body will express it with illnesses, your brain will express it with sadness, anger, even depression. The saving grace is, you can take charge and treat love as a doctor treats your body. As doctors practice proper treatment, study love, then prescribe the right process for yourself to create a healthy love life. My job is to be your guide through the process.

I wrote this simple book to describe *true love* as it has existed since the creation of the universe. Most religious missions lean into it. However, little explanation of what it actually is and how you can benefit from it has ever been organized and presented publicly, that I know of.

- This book illustrates the application of my analysis, presented in the story of how I got to know the right person for me.

- Your Case for Love gives you guidance on how to find the right person for you and processes to practice that will help you keep the relationship enjoyable.

- The introduction shares examples of self, intimate and community love action takers.

How to Use This Book

First, read the foreword and introduction. You'll get a better feel for who I am by reading the foreword, written by someone who knows me very well, my wife. Born in New York and raised in Michigan, she's as straightforward as they come.

The following are answers to questions you may have now and as you read *Your Case for Love*:

- What you learn in *Your Case for Love* is stronger than depression and anxiety and may help overcome them.

- Read from the front to back, in order.

- In contrast, I arrived at the structure for this book backwards. The podcast section came first, then it revealed to me that it needed more explanation, so I ventured to tell the Your (my) Case for Love *story*.

- The story shares action items. You'll want to take notes. Start practicing what you learn right away.

- I suggest you do not read the book in one setting. Instead, flow with the lessons.

When you get to the insight, put the book down for a day or more.

- Allow the lesson you absorbed to linger and repeat in your mind like the last words of a song right before you've turned the radio off. Then move on.

- For the best results, make each lesson a habit by keeping a list in the journal in the back of the book and consciously repeating them.

- To help shift your mindset, love is not outside of yourself, think of it from a provisional perspective.

- After completing #YourCaseforLove, claim your new knowledge as a #YourCaseforLove ambassador, by posting using the hashtags in this sentence #MyCaseforLove. All are yours to use freely.

Liz

Foreword

I'll admit it. I'm biased towards Tony. In a good way! You see, I'm his wife. We met the modern way, online, in October of

2008. By March of 2009 we were married. Crazy, right? Well, maybe, but we both live by the motto of "seize the moment," because life is just too darn short. The truth is we each had great clarity about the kind of person we were looking for, so it

was easy to spot it in each other from our lists. We were each looking for a partner who was compassionate, respectful, concerned with the well-being of others, faithful, a curious learner, health-conscious and with a growth mindset.

Tony has each of those characteristics, with his most innate trait being that of compassion. His love of other people is unbounded and he knows, like you know, that the way to create healing in our world is through compassionate care for others. That will look different for every person, of course. Your ability to care for others is different than mine. The important point being to take action.

Now, Tony's certainly not alone in compassionately caring for the needs of others. What is unique about Tony are his teachings. This book tells his personal story, sure, but it goes above and beyond that to share actionable steps anyone can take to demonstrate true love to your fellow human beings.

The word "love" is too often confused with lust, and after reading this book you'll be clear on the difference and have strategies for showing more love, more often to others. The side effect? You'll find a deeper sense of love for yourself.

As a couple, Tony and I now consistently live by each of these 14 love lessons. Some came easy to us and some were born out of mistakes and pain. Hindsight is 20/20 and it is my hope that by reading this book you'll benefit from our experiences.

As a licensed clinical social worker with over 21 years of master's level experience and having worked with populations from juvenile delinquents in residential facilities to active-duty service members and their families, I can tell you one thing that all hurting people have in common. They all want to feel heard and know that we have their best interests in mind. Let's face it, there are a lot of hurting people in our world right now, and it's likely to get worse before it gets better. Do what you can to make a positive difference when you can. Use this book as a guide for #ACaseforLove #YourCaseforLove #MyCaseforLove

Elizabeth L. Merriweather L.C.S.W., practicing psychotherapist (virtually) in Pensacola, Florida. Also licensed to practice in Michigan, Connecticut, Massachusetts and Tennessee. Co-author of *The Ultimate fitness Workbook* and *Everything Cacao for Diabetics*. Certified American Diabetes Association mindfulness provider.

CLICK THE VIDEO ABOVE TO LISTEN
TESTIMONIAL FROM RELATIONSHIP COACH, CHERYL MUIR

"I've been there. I remember dating the same person over and over again. The same cycle of unavailable men, my obsessions, and the inevitable heartbreak that would follow.

I read all the dating books. Applied all of the dating strategy. Said the "right" thing. Waited to text back. Tried on this "feminine energy" thing.

Tony's book is going to help lot's and lot's of people!

Note about the **<u>table of content</u>**

If you were emailed a download because you purchased the book from my site, <u>click</u> the number in the table of content to get to the page of your desire.

Content

Note from the Author 9

How to Use This Book 11

Liz   14

Foreword 17

Click the video above to Listen 20

Testimonial from Relationship Coach, Cheryl Muir...20

Note about the table of content:....21

New Section 1

Introduction..8

Who This Book Is For 10

Three Cases for Love 12

1. Community Love:..............................12

2. Romantic Love: 13

3. Self-Love:..14

What You Get Out of This Book 18

Inspired by the Historic Time of COVID-19 and Black Lives Matter 22

Chapter 1 Believe 26

Lesson 1: Personality Truths 29

Exercise: 29

Chapter 2 No Matter What, Respect 32

Lesson 2: Respect Opposing Opinions 37

Takeaway: 38

Questions: 38

Chapter 3 Lust 42

Lesson 3: Lust Is Not Love. It Has Its Own Definition. 43

Lust (Wikipedia) 43

Takeaway: 44

Questions: 44

Chapter 4 Create Your List 46

Excerpts from My List: 46

Lesson 4: Treat Others Like You Expect to Be Treated 51

Exercise: 51

Question: 52

Task: 52

Chapter 5 Why Use a Filter? 54

Lesson 5: Feelings Are Fickle, They'll Fool You. .57

Question: 58

Chapter 6 60

Expectations Conversations 60

Lesson 6: Plan Expectations Conversations 65

Question: 65

Chapter 7 68

Speak Your Thoughts 68

Lesson 7: Honesty Is Always the Best Policy 74

Question: 74

Chapter 8 Our Life Partner Plan 76

Excerpts from Our Life Partner Plan 77

Our escape ladder: 79

Lesson 8: Reach for Understanding 83

Exercise: 83

Read the blog post, then write a list of Chainversation points you may need to begin and revisit in the back of this book. 83

Chapter 9 The Recorded Introduction......86

Lesson 9: 89

True Love (tru luv) v. 89

Lesson 10a: Love Is Giving 91

Assignment: 91

Chapter 10 Take Responsibility...............92

Lesson 10b: Refrain from Blame.......................95

Takeaway: 95

Exercise: 95

Chapter 11 Live the Love You Want........98

This is fact:.......................................101

Lesson 11: Live the Love You Want 103

Question: 103

Chapter 12 What Can I Do to Make Your
Life Better?..106

Lesson 12: Enabling is not Love. 109

Questions: 109

An anonymous inquirer asked; 111

Chapter 13...114

True Love Is Not Toxic or Dangerous 114

The Plan: 116

Suggested Response:.................................116

Lesson 13: The Most Important Thing. 119

Exercise: 119

Suggested categories:..............................120

Chapter 14 Love Is the Priority...............122

Lesson 14: Cooperate to Support People 125

Exercise: 125

Liz through the ages 127

Cherokee Park walking areas 129

Conclusion...**132**

Our best to you! Tony and Liz 2010 134
Sources and Resources.........................**135**
My List Qualities in my partner **137**

Journal **139**

Suggested category For myself or....139
For my partner or 141
For children or 143
For extended family or 145
For my parents or..............................147
For people I pass on the street or.....149
For co-workers or 151
For employees and contractors or....153
To help create a loving world or 155
For teachers or...................................157
For care providers or.........................159
For service workers or 161
For drivers on the road or 163
For people who aren't like me or 165
People who believe different or.........167
For 169
For 171
For 173
For 175
For 177

For 179

For 181

For 183

For 185

For 187

Expectations Conversations Points ..189

Expectations Conversations Points ..190

For 191

For 193

For 195

For 197

For 199

For 201

For 203

For 205

For 207

For 209

For 211

For 213

For 215

About me, the author 217

https://www.yourcaseforlove.com..........................220

Contact 222

Get my coaching 222

Introduction

This book is about the power of love that lives in you. If you are to have strong love in your life, have it serve you and those around you with its super power, it's extremely important that you separate the meaning of love from lust.

The word love has been substituted for lust for too long. It's time love takes its true place. That's why in this book, we'll call it "*True Love*."

Don't get it twisted, lust (sexual attraction) is a human emotion that must be recognized and has its place as well. It must be allowed to flow *appropriately*. However, we know it has been and continues to be misused. More on this in pages ahead.

☑ As you move ahead, make building the skill of *listening* your highest priority.

Who This Book Is For

This book is for individuals looking to minimize the possibilities of entering another failing relationship. This book is guidance for selecting a partner to win with.

Whether you're just starting your dating search or you've been at it for a while, male, female, LGBT, older or just out of high school, married, single, spiritual seeker, religious, this book will be a new way of thinking for you. It will guide you, the intimate relationship seeker, through finding that close to just right person and developing a great relationship with them, or strengthening the one you're already in.

Keep in mind, there are no perfect people to choose from, but you can get as close as 97%, maybe as close as 99% of your desired choice if you're patient.

If you haven't made a choice yet, good! I suggest reading this book first. Then go through the course with the person you decide to walk the path of *Life* with.

Three Cases for Love

1. Community Love:

I started in the school system as a teacher assistant. Several years after my song's regional radio hit, I returned as a teacher assistant. The following year my four-year-old multiple sclerosis student and I hung out as she learned to walk with me. Then my principal drafted me as the lead teacher of my own class. I was eligible because of the number of credits I'd earned, though I had yet to finish college. At the end of that year, my principal and I walked the halls talking. She informed me that my students had made the highest percentage of progress in the entire school.

"How did you do it?" she asked.

I care about the well-being of each and every student, so I get to know them. That allows me to recognize their unique gifts and talents. I then encourage those gifts and invite the parents into the process by calling them each night to let them know what we're working on. I ask for their help with each topic. I call it love.

2. Romantic Love:

On her routine doctor visit, the only person in the waiting room, the receptionist called her right after she signed in. After sitting with the doctor a few minutes, the door opened. She walked to the window to wait for her prescription. Depression plagued her. Her relationship of over twenty years had worn her thin. There was no love left to get or give.

She thought she'd made all the right choices: college, a husband, children, church, charity, doing her best to be a good person. It didn't matter. It wasn't enough. As fate would have it, she left the relationship, found a new one and in a few short years was off the medication. It wasn't a miracle. She'd married a health-conscious man who'd learned the concepts I'm about to share with you in this book. They mixed these concepts with a clean, nutritious diet and a focus on the work she loves, helping people. The results, in her own words: "I've never been happier."

3. Self-Love:

Teacher, curriculum writer, community development program creator, conflict resolution workshop presenter, I've helped people over the last forty-five years in some way or another.

Today my wife takes one end of the court and I the other, and we go hard one-on-one fast paced basketball, running from rim to rim. I have to admit, she's a great shot and wins a lot. It wasn't always like that. Years before, after a car accident left me in the hospital in a two-week coma, the doctors predicted that I'd never walk again nor be able to learn any more than I knew at the time. That I would become a vegetable.

I applied the concepts in this book to myself, putting every waking hour into learning what I needed to become strong enough to walk again. I earned a 4.0 in college. That kind of personal development comes with as much work as it does self-love, true love. Then I applied the concepts in Your Case for Love to my twelve years of blissful marriage.

Because of the need for love in our society, I originally wrote this book for business owners and professionals, for non-profit workers, and individuals who've dedicated a big portion of their lives to helping others, and introverted empaths like myself. Individuals looking to minimize the possibilities of entering another failing or toxic relationship and selecting a partner to win with, this book is for you. Couples who argue will find it very helpful. Since the time of its original writing I've narrowed the focus, because I know gratified couples help bring joy into this world.

I'd planned to write this book for my media training and interview course. I coach my students to practice achieving a natural presentation. There is a component within that course that helps guide students through raising funds for their cause or non-profit that helps people. Then I thought, *"Wait a minute! Everybody needs love! The book should be available to anyone who wants a copy."*

I wished an older person would've guided me into knowledge and wisdom as a pre-teen. As I've matured, I'm committed to treating people the way I want to be treated and enjoy sharing the knowledge and experiences I've learned. Extract and document the tips throughout this book.

What You Get Out of This Book

Consider *Your Case for Love* your bypass guide.

Many major cities around the world have what is called a bypass. A **bypass** is a road or highway that avoids or "bypasses" a built-up area, town, or village, to let through traffic flow without interference from local traffic, to reduce congestion in the built-up area, and improve road safety.

When you've finished reading *Your Case for Love*, and have put in place the mindset it encourages, when you understand and practice the processes and procedures illustrated in the story and the love lessons, you will have programmed your emotional and relationship Global Positioning System (GPS) to guide you away from, or around toxic relationships, directing you toward your destiny of a most satisfying relationship.

You will be prepared to find and be with the one person you want to be with forever. Getting the mindset and techniques in *Your Case for Love* down first will better prepare you to love all other humans.

- *Your Case for Love* has 14 lessons in love and love action items. The lessons follow the form of the story, but are not necessarily grouped into categories such as romantic love, community love, etc. I left them as simply *true love*.

- Chapters end with lessons from the previous or following section and include a story, takeaway or action item.

- Expect to see love referenced with spiritual leaders and scriptures.

Love is a commitment that will help you lift yourself and those you care for through the hardest of times. If you can't stand references to spiritual leaders and scriptures, *Your Case for Love* may not be for you. If you are ready to put to practice a love that is designed to develop strong relationships, build you up and everyone you come in contact with, then you'll want to read every word of *Your Case for Love*.

I want to take this space to thank my wife for taking time out of her busy schedule to assemble a foreword for this work.

Thanks to my editor, Jacquelin Cangro for her wisdom and guidance in helping me get through the writing and accepting the job of editing the book.

Inspired by the Historic Time of COVID-19 and Black Lives Matter

I thought you should know, the following was the book's beginning, before I added my personal story.

My podcasting slammed to a stop May 25th, 2020. Painfully, emotional tears streamed from my eyes. As I watched the slow murder of George Floyd, I screamed, "Why? Why? Why?"

My mind and body reacted as though my mother had died a second time, or my brother was brought to life and shot in the head again. I hurt! Bad. Those nine minutes of watching him tied and choked launched my empathic soul into weeks of inconsolable crying. I was paralyzed. Day after day, I couldn't work.

Police were attacking black people with batons, their dogs biting them. She looked at me and with burning anger in her eyes gushed out,

"I never want to watch another racist African American movie or documentary again. They're too depressing!"

We visited Lorraine hotel in Memphis Tennessee to see where Dr. Martin Luther King was shot. The Cadillacs were still sitting in the parking lot under the room. We'd visited Stax museum and Sun Recording studios where my mother had recorded.

Because Liz came from an almost totally white city, she wanted to learn more about history as it relates to me, but I never saw that statement coming. She was deeply angered by the treatment of black people she'd seen in those movies and documentaries.

We've since come to agree that more people need to understand and act on the solution. I met the woman I'm referring to online in October of 2008. I was so excited. The following chapters demonstrate how it started and what followed.

Chapter 1
Believe

If you haven't read my note to you, the forward and the introduction to page 23, please go back and read those sections.

It was a quiet, beautiful sunny day. My bus driving skills were guiding a 20-foot U-Haul back to my hometown after a few months' stay in Michiana, the RV capital when my mother called. Though my life is still in transition, I'll share the following fourteen simple but effective lessons I've learned through the years.

Just to familiarize you with Michiana, it's the corner where Indiana and Michigan touch near Illinois. If you're fascinated with horse and buggy,

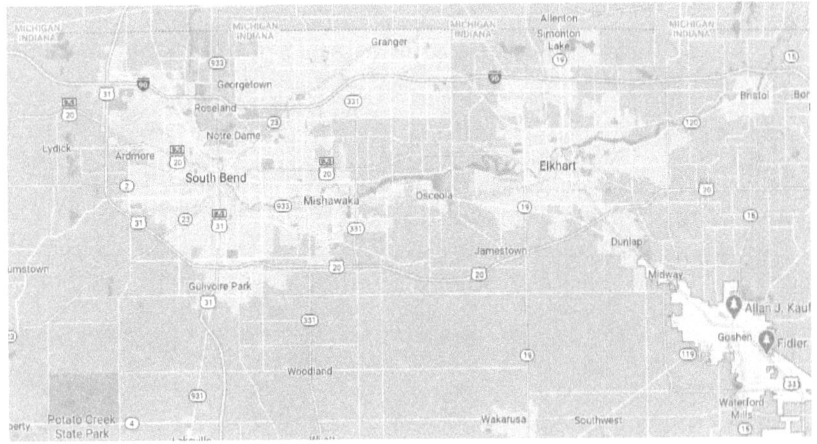

think about touring the Amish and Mennonite communities of Goshen, Indiana.

Before moving there, I'd recently finished work on my business degree. I had hopes of entering a lasting, supportive, loving relationship. I may have been afraid it would never happen. I wanted so much to be in a great relationship. Truth is, I had been conditioned to think no one would treat me good.

Trying to hold back my tears and drive, I couldn't believe what just happened. It was going to be a long drive back to the city.

I was boiling angry. The lady I moved there for told me a truck driver that she worked with had asked her on a date. I thought things were fine between us. It turned out she'd been wanting to date him. That was her calling to break up with me.

Don't feel bad for me. She was one of the worst screamers I'd ever encountered. I just felt so disrespected that she couldn't keep our commitment. I've never been one to try to convince a woman to stay when she wanted to go. Besides, it was my own fault.

My relationships have been a series of start out good then grow to terrible experiences. It's like I couldn't discern people who could only care about themselves.

Lesson 1:
Personality Truths

Believe a person is who they are when they tell you. During our chats she told me about the time she'd beat a woman off a bar stool. I asked her why she did it. She said,

"I'm bi-polar, so when I caught her flirting with my husband one too many times, I let her have it."

I was given this *personality truth* lesson time after time. Had I paid attention to the advice, I would have never gone there. It wasn't until I was ready to hold myself accountable that I'd do what I knew. That time wasn't here but was coming.

Exercise:

Ask friends to tell you a story of what made them, to conclude with who they are. Then use every opportunity to engage in a *practice* of believing their *personality truth* to be who they say they are.

This is a super powerful way to practice identifying personal qualities that resonate with you or repulse you in new people you meet.

Click the link or copy and paste to see what your abundant love archetype is: https://www.yourcaseforlove.com/take-the-quiz-thanks

Then take the *Right Person Challenge* at the end of the book.

It's easier to make intelligent choices and move away from dangerous emotional choices when you apply the techniques in *Your Case for Love.* More to come!

The Takeaways, Lessons, Exercises and Tasks may sound simple, but don't move to the next chapter until you've taken at least a day to practice each lesson.

Chapter 2
No Matter What, Respect

Mom's name popped up in my phone's ID bar and I cheered up.

"How are you momma dear?"

She said, "I'm fine Jack! I should be asking how you're doing!"

I had attended my aunt's funeral not too long before moving to Michiana.

She said, "Your uncle's not doing well. If you don't mind, I'd like you to pull your truck up over there and stay with him a while. Help him out."

The break-up was abrupt. There wasn't time to schedule an interview with anyone. All I had time to do was get to the U-Haul dealer, get my things and go. I wanted out of there as quick as I could get loaded up. I hadn't checked with my old landlord to see if I could get an apartment advance. I needed a place to stay. I said, "I'll do it."

She said, "Thanks, I'll let him know."

We hung up and my mind started racing, wondering what was ahead. My aunt kept the house nice and clean and it was in a nice neighborhood, so I felt good.

When I got there, he had me back the truck down to the basement's garage door and prepare to unload the next morning. He said, "You've had a long ride, come in and get something to eat and rest."

I parked the truck, put the lock on the back, locked it and walked up the steps to the front door. Three big dogs stood at the screen door barking at me. Please believe me: I'm not a fan of big dogs looking like they want to chew on my tissue!

He screamed and pointed, "Go sit down!"

They all ran to the TV room and jumped in the two chairs that sat in front of the television. He came back, opened the door, and said, "They won't bite, come on in."

I walked in behind him to dog hair on the bottom of the walls. It looked like a carpet of dog hair on the floor of the entire house. This was where I would now reside. Mom was right. My uncle wasn't feeling well. I had promised Mom I would help him and I was happy to be there.

He introduced me to the room with a bunk bed I'd be staying in: his stepdaughter's, who was away at college. A computer sat on a desk in the corner. YES! It had the internet! He would sit there and play games for hours.

When he left the room, I'd take a seat and log into match.com and Christian Mingle. It seemed that every relationship I'd been in previously was the worst I'd been in. The truth was, we just didn't get along because I made relationship choices for the wrong reason, lust. I was determined that this time was going to be different. I knew meeting in person could spark flames and one thing lead to another. So I purposely pursued online dating.

Since a break-up at sixteen years old, I wanted to be the type of guy a woman would be grateful to be with. So I worked on my mindset daily. My focus, *How can I make your life better?* That always seemed to send the wrong message though.

I got that idea from reading about Gandhi, Martin Luther King Jr, and the life of Jesus Christ. Jesus walked the earth answering that question with everyone he met, before he was attacked. Even after. I'll talk about this in more detail later in the book.

From early in life, I've always wanted to be able to treat a woman in ways that she would know she's loved. I wanted her to be pleased that a man would treat her with golden noble respect, supporting her dreams and desires. To do that I needed to understand true love, so I started my research at a very young age.

My commitment was to get to know the opposite sex as friends. Get to know what they like and dislike. Understand what ticks them off and what excites them. Just be friends.

I held to the understanding that friends will be honest with you because they have no reason to fill your head up with impressions that they are more than who they are, or that they feel more about you than they really do.

Lesson 2:
Respect Opposing Opinions

I had a habit. Before I moved away, I lived in a green community, next to a five-mile around park. It was practically my backyard. The park had roads going up and around in it, which made the travel through it much longer than five miles. My habit was getting up each morning to jog around that park. Many days I'd take the challenge, running up the roads inside of it.

My uncle was near fifty-five and had acquired diabetes over the years. Each day I'd ask, "Let's go jogging!"

"Nah, I'm okay without all that."

I'd say, "I'm good with walking, let's do that!"

Each time I'd ask, he'd reply, "Nah, I'm okay without all that."

I wouldn't push, although my research told me he could possibly reverse his diabetes by exercising and eating clean. He was doing himself a disservice by doing neither.

Takeaway:

Never assume that because you know what you offer a person is good for them, that they should be obligated to accept your offer. A better approach is to be open to their response. Whatever it is, respect it.

Questions:

1. Can you recall a time when you felt you knew what was best for another person

2. How can you encourage yourself not to project your thoughts on another's decision(s)?

Goals

Olympia

Chapter 3
Lust

Jogging around the neighborhood, cleaning the kitchen, checking wanted ads, sending resumes and making friends on match.com and Christian Mingle became my daily routine.

During my exercise I would absorb thoughts and develop ideas. One of those ideas was to write down my desires. I wanted to steer myself away from choosing a partner from lust alone.

Of course, sexual attraction had to be a factor, but we're probably going to spend about 4% of our time being intimate. What would we do the other 96% of the time?

I wanted to etch out a three-dimensional vision of who my wife would be. So I started creating a list of my desires.

Lesson 3: Lust Is Not Love. It Has Its Own Definition.

Definition of *lust*. (Entry 1 of 2)

1: usually intense or unbridled sexual desire : lasciviousness. *He was motivated more by* **lust** *than by love.*

2a: an intense longing : craving a **lust** to succeed. 2b : enthusiasm, eagerness, *admired his* **lust** *for life.*

Lust (Wikipedia)

Lust is a psychological force producing intense desire for an object, or circumstance fulfilling the emotion while already having a significant other or amount of the desired object. **Lust** can take any form such as the **lust** for sexuality (see libido), love, money, or power.

Contrary to what many teach, lust is not a bad thing in and of itself. It becomes a bad thing when it isn't understood for what it is, and is allowed to be the center focus out of context, or when it's used as a decision-making tool.

Takeaway:

Word Substitution Causes Confusion

Questions:

1. Do you currently have a habit of using substitute words for sex, lust and love?

2. How easy will it be for you to adapt the real words for sex, lust and love? Declare it here.

Chapter 4
Create Your List

Physical attraction should never be used as the primary decision-maker when it comes to choosing a mate. A list can help guide you to making better decisions, and away from them being based solely on the physical.

EXCERPTS FROM MY LIST:

Number one! She had to be able to talk through every problem with me to a conclusion that both of us could be comfortable with, without yelling. If there's boiling anger, we both needed to be able to walk away. Coming back to it to reach a conclusion is a must.

2. We must have a close understanding of the purpose of lust and agree on what love is.

3. She must be able to speak her thoughts without feeling like she has to shake her finger at me and *Give me a piece of her mind!*

4. She had to be compassionate and care about the well-being of other people.

5. She had to care enough about other people to want to help people on a large scale.

6. She had to be familiar with starting a business from the ground up, or at least comfortable with me doing so.

7. She had to be able to sit down and create frequent plans with me.

8. I'd dreamed I'd marry a tall woman with red hair and grey temples. That became my desire!

You probably think I'm super picky. I'm actually not. I'd just grown frustrated with myself because I never seemed to pick the right person. I felt like there was THAT *right person* in the world, from the depths of my heart, the one who got me. The woman who understands it when I feel the need to work on projects morning to night through that project's development. The woman who could listen to me talk about my ideas and not say, "That's crazy," or

"How do you expect to pull that off ?"

I'll tell you something that not many people know about me.

At sixteen, my girlfriend broke up with me a few days before Christmas. I kept thinking, *She's kidding, she's going to surprise me and show up Christmas day.* She didn't. I laid across my bed crying for hours thinking of ways I could kill myself. Should I borrow Mom's car and drive it into the river? Should I fall on a knife? Should I run in front of a speeding truck? I couldn't. I felt like I would leave my mother in so much pain.

I had been teased so much by my friends and family simply because I'm different. I'm an inventive artist. I would feel so unwanted, so I'd spend my time away from them, creating.

I felt people simply liked hurting my feelings. They enjoyed making me feel terrible. Some would even laugh at me about it.

I wanted to show people how to treat me. That seemed to start a track playing in the back of my mind. When everything else stopped it said, *"What can I do to help make your life better?"* Like the universe was speaking to me from inside my head. It became a mantra in my life. It worked on me, while it helped me focus the same thought on other people.

I wanted a woman to be totally happy with me. So I felt it was more important for me to learn how to make sure I treated people with love. It was important for me that they know they are loved. It was even more important than earning money.

Lesson 4: Treat Others Like You Expect to Be Treated

How do you view other people, from the top of your list to the bottom, from appreciated to despised?

As an empath, I hurt when others hurt and I can't help but feel the joy and celebrate the accomplishments and good deeds of others. One of my uncles told me,

"You are the other person to other people."

I had been treating everyone else better than I treated myself. With my uncle's lesson in mind, it became extremely important that I learn to apply True Love as it is described in this book to myself first, then treat others as I treat myself. Not better, but as good.

Exercise:

Draw a line down the center of an untitled *journal page* in the back of this book. On the *left side* write things you've done to people that you wouldn't want done to you. Be honest, you may be the only one to see this.

On the *right side* write treatments, or benefits you've felt you deserved but did not receive them. This may actually take several pages.

Question:

How can you exclude the left side and actualize the right side for people whose path you cross?

Task:

Start your, "Qualities in my partner" list on that page in the back of this book. (Check the table of content)

Chapter 5
Why Use a Filter?

Back to my super picky search.

I would click and read profiles to uncover some similarities of the lady on my list. I bet I'd clicked over a hundred women, or more. I would request online chats when I noticed even the slightest match. I'd go on meet-ups after chatting with them several days to feel like we knew each other. The same old problem kept showing up: we'd meet, attraction showed up, they'd claim relationship and I'd say, "No, we're friends."

Then one day I said, "No, I'm not doing this anymore." I'm only looking for the one person who fits my list. I let go of the comparability mindset and adapted the focused mindset. The most important thing on my list was that she solve problems without yelling. So I started asking that question in chats. Not one could agree.

One day as I scrolled, I noticed a tall woman with blond hair posing for the picture with her sister, daughter and a larger French Brittany. I clicked the profile to read about her. I was determined not to settle for less than what was on my list. I started to click away when I read she worked for the government. I did not want to meet a soldier because life could be uncertain, and I didn't want a police officer because she could be mean. Curious as to what her job was, I continued to read. I read every word she had on the site. She'd laid her job description out pretty clear.

Now that I knew she wasn't a soldier or a police officer, I stopped reading and clicked to scroll through her pictures. I was happy there were no bikini shots. Then a picture opened that showed her peachy skin, one side, her hip. My heart jumped! Whoa! I really needed to turn away! Lust had grabbed a hold of me. I went back to read more about her. I'm a hips man. I couldn't help thinking about the picture I just saw. So I decided to request her permission to message her. I made a commitment that if she accepted, I'd stop all other search communications.

I was sixteen when I started touring, singing and playing music with a band, years before she and I met online. I was burned out by the time I was actually old enough to be in night clubs. I wanted to learn to produce music and write for other artists. So I started junior college. After three years of paying my way through junior college music school, I earned a scholarship to Berklee College of Music.

I turned down two offers while in Boston. The first was to move to Alabama and write for Muscle Shoals Studio. The second was to sing on a Marvin Gaye remake and tour Puerto Rico performing with my teacher.

Both offers just didn't feel right, so I moved back to my home town. Had I accepted either of those offers, I may have never taught school, had the opportunity to help a little girl learn to walk, or meet Liz. I was twenty-five and it was during those times that my compassionate mindset began to strengthen. It was during that time that I really began to understand true love.

Lesson 5: Feelings Are Fickle, They'll Fool You.

Think of feelings as a compass. They show up to point you in a direction where to get information. Instead of rushing to get in, seek out as many facts as you can ahead of time before you arrive. This information will empower you to make the best decision. No one knows the future. However, facts will help you prepare for what's down the road.

Once you have your desires list, it's time to get information. Get to know people, no commitment yet. Talk. Get the facts, not *things in common*, but actual natural behaviors and personality traits. I

chose a dating site purposefully to keep our hands and lips off each other while we gave ourselves time to get to know each other.

Question:

How will you maintain your distance while getting to know people?

____

____

____

____

____

____

____

____

____

____

____

____

Chapter 6
Expectations
Conversations

She was 46, I was 49 and excited to hopefully get a message from Liz the next day. I checked my box and—ta da! —she'd written. It wasn't much. I was just happy to have the opportunity to chat with her. I liked everything I saw and read about her, and her hips. 😊 She had a master's degree in social work.

I could see Jeffersonville, Indiana across the river from my home in Kentucky. She lived in a suburb an hour north of Detroit, which kept us a great distance from one another. She answered my question about solving our problems by saying she hates yelling. She played piano and clarinet and her son was a bass player. As a composition major and keyboard player, I felt we'd have a ball together.

I'd recently written my first novel based on a community music program I'd created. We chatted about that and how I had defined love. (Actually, I

hadn't defined love, I transcribed the definition from another source I'll share later.)

One day she and I were chatting back and forth and I asked, "If you were cooking and I approached you from behind and hugged you, how would you respond?"

She wrote, "I hope you'll let me know so I can hug you back. Plus, I love me some chocolate cake!" I typed, "I do too! Wow! How coincidental is that!" I had no idea that was a hint!

A few weeks had passed since we met when she wrote, "I'll be coming to your city soon. Would you like to meet in person?"

"Yes, I would," I replied. As soon as those words left my fingers, yellow nervousness rushed

through me as if it was standing next to me waiting to hurry and take over my body. She gave me the date she would arrive. We planned a coffee meet-up in a month. The countdown was on.

Shortly after we set the date, I got a phone call from an employer, a manufacturer of professional sportswear. They offered me the job. I'd now be responsible for helping outfit 158 professional sports teams, 149 U.S. and 9 Canadian. The work was seasonal, but I was on my way to productivity. This couldn't have come at a better time! I'd been sleeping on the cement basement floor, because my cousin had returned from school.

I felt guilty asking. I love my uncle. I knew where I could find him when I needed to talk. I walked to the TV room, with my heart in my hand

and told him, "I just got hired to do jersey production work. Liz is coming to visit in a month. I want to have a place to take her."

He said, "You can bring her here."

Feeling guiltier, I said, "I think she's going to want to be alone. I need to get an apartment. Are you okay with being here alone?"

"Do what you gotta do!" he said.

"Alright. Are you able to drop me at work today?"

"Don't I always take you?! Let me know when you're ready."

I turned and made my way to the basement, where I had set up my computer, and started my apartment search. Then it hit me! What was I thinking? I wasn't. I started going through my contacts to pull Jan up, my old landlord. I clicked the number. Two rings and she picked up.

"Hi Jan! It's Tony."

"Hi Tony! So you're back in town?"

"Yep. It didn't work so well there. Do you have an apartment available?"

"Absolutely. There's a first floor available with the front windows facing the parkway."

"Great, let's schedule a visit."

I'd sold my car before I moved away, so I borrowed my uncle's S.U.V. to meet Jan the next day. It was perfect: in the magnificently green neighborhood I'd lived in before, full of large Victorian style homes with the gigantic park literally right outside my front door. I put my deposit down.

Though I had a place, I continued to stay with my uncle and pay him rent. My job was down the street from where he lived. It was much easier for me to get to work from his house than catching a city bus two hours early from my apartment forty-five minutes across town.

Lesson 6: Plan Expectations Conversations

Based on my psychology studies and personal experience, expectations are the number two cause of relationship breakdowns, behind unfaithfulness. Entering into a relationship

1. *without* taking time to get to know the person's natural behaviors as a friend first, or

2. without planning to sit down together on a scheduled or consistent basis to discuss differences and expectations is a formula for disaster. S/he may expect you to hang your coat and put your shoes in the closet when you enter home. You were never told, as a result, s/he's angered each time you do different. No two people grew to hold the same expectations. That's why it's a must to have hard, expectations conversations.

Question:

What are some obvious expectations you have that could be different than people you meet? Write them in the back of this book.

A few doors down

Chapter 7
Speak Your Thoughts

Liz called. "You'll have to guide me to where you are. I'm just crossing the bridge into your city."

"What highway are you on?"

"I'm on 65 South"

"I'll stay on with you. You're going to stay on 65 South until you see I-264. Take the west exit to Dixie Highway south and I'll guide you from there."

Wow! The day was finally here! I was super nervous. You could probably launch a rocket from the blood pumping through my veins. Maybe I shouldn't have, but I told her,

"I'm nervous to meet you!"

"Why? You shouldn't be."

"You're from a totally different side of life than I am. You may meet me and not like me. There are a lot of reasons. I'm from a predominantly black neighborhood, you're from the white suburbs. I could go on, but do you see what I'm saying?"

"Let's meet first. We can see if those things affect us later."

That comment cemented what I'd studied about her and it confirmed my expectations, though I knew better than to place expectations on another person without clarifying with them.

I stood in front of the house as I guided her to me. She parked, got out. She was a well-spoken tall woman with freshly trimmed blond hair and a beautifully white smile.

I wanted to reach out and shake her hand to greet her, but early lessons from my father taught me to allow the woman to greet you in their own way.

"How are you today?" she said as she reached her arms out, inviting me to a hug. I nervously hurried to hold her, but stayed a respectful non-touching midsection distance away.

As she released the grip, I respectfully let go and responded, "I'm fine now that we're finally meeting! Let's go in."

"I've been driving all day. I'd rather stand out here."

"I'd like to introduce you to my uncle. I'll be right back."

"Uncle Owen, meet Liz."

They greeted one another, then she turned to me and asked,

"Are you ready?

We said bye to Uncle Owen, and got in her car. After coffee we rode and talked for hours until dark. I wanted her to meet another uncle, so we needed to find a spot to wait while I tried to get him on the phone.

We parked in the lot of a Barnes and Noble near my younger uncle's home. I turned to look at her.

"He's probably out bowling."

There was a green, yellow and lavender aura glowing around her. My body started buzzing with tingling vibrations stronger than I'd ever felt. My heart felt like it was pumping more powerfully than ever before. A voice inside my head said, "I know you're afraid, but tell her now, or you may never see her again." So I said it.

"You're my wife!"

Things got quiet.

We sat there for a few minutes in the quiet. I assumed she was going to say it was a crazy thought, or that it was too soon to even think about that, or even, "This might need to be over if you're thinking about that this quick."

But she turned to me and asked, "How could you know that?"

I explained her glow and the feeling I had flowing through me. "My feelings had been growing since we decided to connect online. I wanted to wait until we met in person to see how we would respond to each other."

She leaned over and initiated an engaging kiss. Could this be, *Yes, I am your wife?* Talk about mind racing! We disconnected a few minutes later and leaned back in our seats.

"I'm not sure that you're not some kind of psychic or mind reader, but that remains to be seen. Spending some time together will help."

Could this be the beginning of another toxic relationship? Would she join with me in a relationship, then one morning wake up and tell me, "I don't want this any more," like I'd heard before? Would she have me and several other guys strung out between here and Michigan? Scary!

None of those questions had an answer. You can't just ask a person these and expect an honest answer, or can you? A curious sensation overwhelmed me to find out. So I burned the boat and bridge. I'll ask later.

The 5-mile diameter Cherokee Park

My apartment. Willow park was on my block. The next block begins Cherokee Park to the edges.

Lesson 7: Honesty Is Always the Best Policy

Don't allow that voice in your head to convince you to withhold your harmless, true thoughts and feelings from others. Even if you feel they may totally dismiss you, or get angry at what you say, it's best that you know their response sooner than later.

Question:

How can you work on putting honest, difficult thoughts into spoken words?

____

____

____

____

____

____

____

____

____

Chapter 8
Our Life Partner Plan

We met in person in Kentucky, November of 2008. We'd enjoy long walks around the park. That's when she told me she didn't think I'd like grey, so she'd been dying her hair. I said,

"Please let your natural hair grow out." Her hair gradually began to reveal auburn, with grey temples that looked like highlights outlining her face. We stayed in an Elizabethtown hotel together until we married in Michigan in March of 2009. Then we moved to my apartment on the parkway.

She told me she'd like to one day run a virtual business, online and over the phone. I had no idea how, but I promised I'd do all I could to help make it happen. We decided to do much planning. One of the plans was our *life partner plan* we wrote the night of our wedding. We agreed, writing our visions creates precognition, seeing the future.

EXCERPTS FROM OUR LIFE PARTNER PLAN

1. No emotional bonding with another outside of our marriage

2. Strive to maintain emotional intelligence

3. Never make emotional decisions, unless it's sex with each other

4. No sex with anyone outside of our marriage

5. Each day before bed, take a few minutes to ask how the day went, each taking turns

6. Hug before leaving each day, preferably before we leave the bed, unless the other is asleep

7. There are no woman jobs and man jobs around the house. When you see something that needs doing, do it

Arizona, Route 66 and the reservation was in sight!

8. No name calling or blaming

9. Point out the problem without acting on feeling the need to blame

10. Aim for a solution to work towards

11. Whoever is responsible for fixing the problem, take responsibility by acknowledging, "I'll work on that."

12. No yelling at one another

13. If either is at a boiling point of anger, ask for time to cool off and table the conversation, always to return and work to a solution

14. Never tell family members, friends or co-workers our problems

15. Never ask family members, friends or co-workers for advice on fixing our problems

Our escape ladder:

16. Before we ever decide to split, we must have discussed all possible solutions. When we've exhausted our possible solutions, the final step is to hire a marriage counselor, attend every counseling session and create a plan under their guidance

We knew it would be work, but those are just a few excerpts besides areas we'd support each other in, such as growth process visions and daily check-ins on how we're feeling, how the day went, and what we need from each other.

One of the items we added to our To-Do list was *travel*.

From our dating days to the present, travel has always entered our conversation. We both had it in our dating profile.

One day she came home from work and said her co- worker mentioned she could travel and work in other cities. She asked me, "How would you like traveling from city to city, staying in different hotels all the time?"

I answered, "That's what we've always talked about, hitting the road and seeing America!"

She said, "I'd have to switch companies and you'd have to quit work. Are you okay with that?"

"If you're okay with it, then I am. I'll have to get a portable keyboard and microphone to keep busy recording. That would give me more time to focus on website development and helping you get your online business set up. Yeah, I think it would be good for us."

"My supervisor's son works for the other company. I'll get his contact and put in the application."

One evening several weeks later, she came to visit me near the end of my shift. This wasn't unusual, since we'd eat lunch there together most every evening, but this was different. My manager and I were standing outside my station talking when she entered. "Can I interrupt?"

"Sure!" he said."

I know how valuable he's been to you, but I have to ask you to let Tony go. I've been offered a position in Houston and I need him with me."

He stretched his arms wide, stepped back and joked, "I can't stand in the way of that, can I!"

We all cracked up laughing.

He said, "Tony's a great worker and supporter of my move here. I don't want to lose him, but I understand and wish you well in your new job."

Our stay in Houston was full of website building study, tech shopping, Texas barbecue dinners, meeting fantastic people and much driving. Her new position was a recruit center counselor, so five days a week, she'd invite me to drive, visit recruit center locations in cities outside Houston and explore the area. Texas is a gigantic, wide highway state.

Taking the back roads when we could, we'd drive for miles some days, sightseeing. Meetings only lasted up to about two hours. We'd leave at 9:00am and our hotel manager wouldn't greet us back until 6:00pm at times. Days were so chopped up. It became necessary to document where we left off in conversations, so we could pick up again later.

Lesson 8:
Reach for Understanding

Our chainversations developed out of necessity. As a psychotherapist, Liz developed the concept into strategically applying *chainversations.*

Like writing a book, or building a house, complicated issues are generally not solved in one conversation, but rather a series of conversations a.k.a. *Chainversations.*

Chainversations are a powerful tool to use in the tough *expectations conversations*. They give you and your partner the time needed to completely express and understand each others thoughts and background.

Exercise:

Read the blog post, then write a list of *Chainversation points* you may need to begin and revisit in the back of this book.

Click 21st Century Communication or copy and paste
http://rhyzemusic.co/21st_Century_Communication

Saint Charles Lewis & Clark exhibit pictures by
Liz and Tony Dee

LEWIS & CLARK MONUMENT
DEDICATED
MAY 18, 2003

After nearly two centuries, the 1804 Corps of Discovery Commanders are back in the City of Saint Charles. In 1993 a group of area citizens decided that Missouri needed a larger than life monument to serve as a tribute to the expedition, and work began to select an artist. Once commissioned, it took the artist Pat Kennedy about 16 months to complete a 15 foot bronze monument of the famed explorers Captain Meriwether Lewis (right), Captain William Clark (left) and Lewis' Newfoundland Dog "Seaman" (center). This monument is dedicated to the memory of Lewis & Clark and the brave men of the Corps of Discovery, as a reminder of their courage. May it serve as an inspiration for all!

LEWIS & CLARK MONUMENT CITIZEN STEERING COMMITTEE

LEO F. BAHR	SUE KURTZ HOEHN	MIKE DEVANEY	CHUCK GROSS	SHIRLEY HUTCHINS
MIMI JACKSON	LOUIS LAUNER	JANE BEASLEY	JOHN DENGLER	ARCHIE SCOTT
LARRY W. HENDERSON	DAN FOUST	GLEN BISHOP	FAWZIA CASTILE	ART CASTILE
FRED J. WAHL	LARRY MUENCH	GENE FITZWALTER	ROBERT MOELLER	MARY ANN OELKLAUS

MAJOR CONTRIBUTORS

STATE of MISSOURI
COUNTY of SAINT CHARLES
SAINT CHARLES CITY PARKS & RECREATION DEPARTMENT

CITY of SAINT CHARLES
MILLSTONE BANGERT, INC.
ST. CHARLES PARKS & RECREATION FOUNDATION

SPECIAL RECOGNITION

ARTIST: PAT KENNEDY - LOVELAND, COLORADO
ART CONSULTANT: STEVE BOODY (BOODY FINE ARTS) - ST. LOUIS, MISSOURI
ARCHITECTURAL DESIGN FIRM: LOOMIS ASSOCIATES - CHESTERFIELD, MISSOURI
RUSTY SAUNDERS - ASLA, DOUGLAS A. DeLONG - ASLA, EDWARD M. DERMODY - ASLA

Chapter 9
The Recorded
Introduction

Houston was just the first stop. That was in 2015. There was Wisconsin, Georgia, Kansas, Arizona, Indiana, and many more. One of our hotels was just a few miles away from the Lewis and Clark Expedition Park in the Saint Charles Settlement on the Missouri River, where we stopped to enjoy a restaurant after my own name.

Because of the amount of free time Liz's job gave her, she started picking up Telemedicine jobs, helping tech geniuses overcome overthinking from wherever we were.

Three years and over two hundred hotel cards later, she'd onboarded nearly enough clients to replace her job income. We decided we'd work from home. Which brings us back to where I left off in the introduction.

My heart still asks the question,

"What can I do to make your life better?"

I live this love with Liz, with my family, my friends, students and clients. May 25th 2020's painful emotional tears screamed at me demanding that I speak the love that had impregnated my life with the significance of its meaning. It insisted that I give birth to its documentation, so as many people as would pick it up, embrace it and live it causing a cognitive reframing in your life and the lives of those you love.

This is a call for you to become something more, to awaken. I wrote this book for you based on a previous podcast episode I'd published. It was a response to George Floyd's murder. Many of the following words were taken from Episode 9 of then titled Love Creativity Podcast, *Love and Black Lives Matter,* (now titled *Your Case for Love* Podcast.

Imagine if every person alive treated each other in the way you'll soon see love defined. Imagine if couples entered into relationships with the understanding and commitment to live in love that way. George Floyd would still be alive today for reasons you'll soon see.

My edited version is as follows:

I was in the shower. And I know you're saying, "I was in the shower too!"

I'm serious. So many ideas flooded my mind that I wanted to share with you. I didn't want to interview anybody. I wanted to talk to you from my heart. This is no script, no bullet points, nothing written down. I'm just sharing my mind with you. We're not only talking about COVID-19 this time. We're talking about Black Lives Matter too.

Recorded podcast introduction:

Your Case for Love

Lesson 9:

When I say love, I'm talking about a love attitude that knows compassion. A love attitude is a love for humanity, for fellow humans, not just romantic or self-love. This is True Love.

True Love (*tru luv*) v.

To feel the need to encourage and lift others up spiritually, psychologically, financially, in wisdom, or action.

2. The unchangeable aspiration that results in a commitment to behave in a lasting effort to serve in ways that are good for, needed by, and in the best interest of the other person or persons.

3. and oneself.

4. It is altruism.

5.It's compassionate, magnanimous behavior.

6.The desire that converts to action to prepare oneself and one's situation to be of the best optimistic benefit for self and others.

7.It is the highest power.

End recorded introduction:

Lesson 10a: Love Is Giving

Therefore, love is *not* possession, obsession, or wantonness. Love takes good care of the people and things it has the freedom to do so.

Assignment:

Below, make a list of as many ways that you can provide for your partner as fits here. Allow your partner to add to your list, then trade places and request they do the same.

____

____

____

____

____

____

____

____

____

____

Chapter 10
Take Responsibility

Although it's related, I'm not talking about Black Lives Matter from a protest standpoint. Years ago, I was pulled over and the cop said,

"You have a light out."

I said, "Okay thanks."

He said, "Give me your license." He checked with the station. He came back and said, "I have to take you up."

"Got to take me up for what?"

"You haven't paid your ticket."

Immediately my temper shot past the ceiling. He handcuffed me, and I kicked my car tire, screaming, "Why are you locking me up? So many people are out here doing crimes. I haven't done nothing! I have to get back home to my daughter and you're locking me up. What is wrong with you man?"

I went to jail. Not only that time. I've been to jail many times for, "You look like the guy that just robbed a store around the corner. We have to take you up for positive ID."

One evening I went out to watch my friend and her new band perform. I was on break from Berklee College of Music. I'd drove my car a little down the street, when "Whoop whoop!" Red and blue lights flashed. I'm sure he smelled cigar smoke, even though I'd let the window down to let it clear.

I said, " Officer sir, I'm here from school staying with my sister. My license is upstairs on her dresser. I forgot them. Can I go get them?"

"No," he replied. "I need to take you to jail for positive ID."

You know, it's been time and time again that we've been going through this. When I kicked my tire, we've seen police officers who would have beat the life out of me. Instead, he was one of the most kind, respectful officers I'd ever met.

This officer displayed an attitude of love. For that reason, I'm still here to tell you about it. The reason is obvious to me. Is it to you? You may not realize how important this thing called love is. It's what I live for. I assume you do as well.

Lesson 10b: Refrain from Blame

Whether you're in an intimate relationship, a friendship, or a business partnership, or you're simply living life, take responsibility for what happens to you. Truth is, the officers may have never taken me to jail had I paid my fines. This is especially important for intimate relationships. When you can avoid attacking each other, name calling or blaming, working through conversations to a solution becomes much easier.

Takeaway:

A solution-centered focus is more useful for solving problems than focusing on a person.

Exercise:

1. Go back in time and write down a list of problems you addressed through focusing on, or blaming the person. Leave space for writing under each.
2. Now with your list in hand, under each, write how you could have focused on getting to the

solution, with no blame.

Chapter 11
Live the Love You Want

Listen to these words deeply. What you'll hear is a detailed description of true love. I didn't make it up. It's not a me thing. As I read the Bible, 1 John 4:16, is really emotional to me.

It reads, "**8** Anyone who does not love does not know God, because God is love. **16** So we have come to know and to believe the love that God has for us. God is love, and *whoever lives in love lives in God, and God lives in him*. **20** If anyone says, "I love God," and hates his neighbor, he is a liar; for he who does not love his neighbor whom he has seen cannot love God whom he has not seen. **21** And this commandment we have from him: whoever loves God must also love his neighbor."

1 John 4:16, "Whoever lives in love lives in God... God lives in us."

It's that electromagnetism that everything in this universe is made of and that holds everything together. It's that energy you feel. God, or *the power of love* allows you to breathe, see, think and do. I'm not trying to preach to you, or push religion on you. I just want to be real with you. I want you to see where I'm coming from.

So the question then becomes, "If love lives in us, what is love?"

We can't see, touch, or definitively hear God. Although we accept that we feel *love's* spirit in our heart, and hear it in our head. What we *can* do, is document and understand *love's* mindset and actions that we can imitate. That's what I did. The outcome was that I documented *love's mindset and behavior.*

See *Your Case for Love*, Lesson 9.

I challenge you to imitate and communicate True Love's mindset and behavior.

First action, God takes darn good care of us. It doesn't matter if we've messed up or not, we get sunshine and rain. We have the ground to walk and build on. Considering that, love must be *taking care of, provision.*

If God, living in us, is love, how can we tune in to it?

We can look at the ways that we can take care of one another. The bottom line is this: it comes down to a commitment to do things that are good for, needed by, and in the best interests of others, ourselves, living beings and our environment. That's what love does.

I want you to really get this because you are so valuable in this world. You are so valuable to not just the people who care about you, but also to the people that you walk past. If you catch their eye and say, "Hi!" or "How are you doing?" you may have just prevented a suicide, or simply derailed a bad day. I'll stop and listen if they want to talk, which many times ends with people saying, "Thanks for taking the time to listen. That made my day!"

On my webpage https://www.yourcaseforlove.com/about-tony-dee, is

"If my eyes meet your eyes, I'm going to say 'hi' to you."

We should all make it a practice. It should be the normal behavior for everyone. I personally would be grateful to see everybody treating each other with respect, love and appreciation, just as we want for ourselves. Would you?

Here's what I don't get. How can a person expect respect and not give it to the next person? Everybody feels the same as you.

THIS IS FACT:

You are the other person to the other person.

Other people look at you, the way you look at them. It's not scientifically proven. However, I can say that and you understand what I'm saying. What you put out, what you give out, what you live, comes back to you.

Search out your own mistakes and atone for them. Be the change you want. When I find myself at odds with my wife or any other person, I ask myself, "What did I do to contribute to this outcome?"

Lesson 11: Live the Love You Want

The same love that lives in you lives in other people. Some know it and show it. Some don't and won't. Your power in love comes in living it. The highest respect you can get comes not in being a threat, earning a degree, or making millions. The highest respect you can get is earned by being an action-taking, loving person.

Question:

How can you condition yourself to respect that love that lives in everyone?

____

____

____

____

____

____

____

Chapter 12
What Can I Do to Make Your Life Better?

L ove has always been the most important thing to me. I was raised in a neighborhood where taking and bullying were easy for people.

I didn't want to, but I learned to fight at a very young age to ward off bullies. I'd wrestle and box a lot with my uncles and many cousins. One uncle used to force me to practice with him on days he'd return from karate school. He called me fast. I've only had a few fights in my life. Thank goodness I never lost. In that type of environment, you sometimes have to say, "Enough is enough."

This thing called life is serious, and we, the human race, really have to get a grip of True Love. Love is the most important aspect of our lives. Think about it.

I'll break it down a little more for you. Traditionally, permission is given after a wedding. In the biblical days, sex, or entering into her, was considered marriage. Love is not, *I want to have sex with you*. Let's be real, that's lust. It's okay, because it's a human quality. But when you are allowed to follow through with your lust with a person, commit. Let it last. Make it real. Give the same respect that you want for yourself.

My words are not meant to preach to you. Just look around. Look at how people are treating others, and have been treating people in ways that they wouldn't want to be treated for years.

It's not just about the black race. A friend told me she walked into a restaurant with her Indian husband and got all kinds of stares. She played with a baby at another table, and the mother turned the baby so she couldn't see. This insensitivity was taught in childhood.

I watched a video of two toddlers, black and white, running towards each other to hug. That kind of concern for the well-being of one another says they were born with the power of love in their hearts.

Here is what the power of love does. It asks, *What can I do to make your life better?*

Whether it's an intimate, professional, or friend relationship, the foundation of a great relationship is based around the question, "*What can I do to make your life better?*"

When both of you marry with the question "*What can I do to make your life better?*" as your commitment, guess what? Your marriage has a chance to last forever. Reach to strengthen your decision-making power beyond, "Ooh, he or she looks good." Commit to that, and you'll create unbreakable bonds.

Another component of our *life partner plan* is *The Escape Ladder*. If it gets so bad that we want to walk away, we've agreed not to just jump. Our agreement is to seek counsel to coach us through to mutually acceptable processes to mend and grow close again. This idea will work for any relationship.

Professional advice is stronger than mind-reading decisions.

Lesson 12: Enabling is not Love.

Enabling is when we do something for another person that they are perfectly capable of doing for themselves. By doing so, we are missing out on our own personal growth and development.

To enable another person might feel like you're helping in the moment, but essentially, it's stunting their growth and development. The relationship then becomes at risk of developing mutual resentments. If you've ever known that experience of feeling like a doormat, it may have been because you were enabling.

When it comes to love, it's important to love both yourself and the other person and consider the best interest of each when making decisions.

Questions:

1. Have you been an enabler?
2. How can you kindly decline the next time?

AN ANONYMOUS INQUIRER ASKED;

"How can I get out of this toxic relationship? When I leave, I always come back, I don't want to live like this anymore. I'm so much in love. Why can't I just leave!"

My answer:

Hold your feelings accountable. Humans are many times more easily addicted to the chemicals that are released from inside our bodies than we are to the substances we put in ourselves.

Anything repeated becomes a way you think. After a period of time, it becomes a habit. With more time passed, it becomes second nature. You get good at it.

You need to give yourself time to get good at being away. That's the only way to break the habit of being there.

By staying in a toxic relationship, or continuing to return, you are enabling them to treat you in the abusive way they've been treating you. It's like you're showing them, *"I like being treated like this."*

Chapter 13
True Love Is Not Toxic or Dangerous

I imagine to avoid embarrassment most men would keep this to themselves. I'll never forget trying to get away from one of the worst relationship experiences of my life. I spent four years under the threat of, "If I can't have you, nobody will." This relationship went from my twenties to my thirties. I remember my walk up a hill on crutches to get away from her. Being popped in the mouth by her, and the grimness of watching her pull her guns trigger aimed at my face.

Each of those incidents were my responsibility.

They were the result of me as an enabler. They were the result of me wanting to *get* more intimacy, instead of doing what I knew was right and loving of myself. At first our relationship seemed wonderful, although I had been warned about her. He used the term *"Man Eater"* to describe her. She treated me with respect and adoration, until we passed the six-month mark.

Then, like clockwork, yelling, screaming and hitting began after the sixth month. I wanted to walk away, explaining to her a couple should be able to work through problems, not battle as if they're enemies.

Mentioning splitting up made her angrier. She told me I was the only thing keeping her sane, so I stayed, to keep her happy. I hoped things would get better. That was toxic optimism.

Each time I accepted this behavior and decided to stay, I enabled that behavior to continue. It was my fault, not hers.

I must tell you, my wife and I have been married going on 13 years. We've gotten so angry with one another that the aftermath could have been many drag-out arguments. Instead, our commitment is to love the way we want to be loved. So when the heat turns up, our plan demands that we don't let problems sit in our head.

The Plan:

Talk; give the other the opportunity to know the problem and work on fixing it.

Suggested Response:
I'll work on that.

- Then we let it go, and trust the work will be done.

- There's no miracle conversation. Chainversations may be necessary. It's okay.

We don't allow each other to hold anger. When we need to talk, we approach each other always in a respectful manner. When my voice gets a little strong, she gently demands that I calm down. I respect that. I love her with all my heart. We are each other's best friends.

Remember she said she didn't want to watch another black documentary. Since George Floyd's departure, she's binged on racial injustice movies and documentaries, history and black stories. It turns out that it would be a crime for a black person to be free in Southern law.

She had no idea our society is still affected by that.

See *Alienable Rights: The Exclusion of African Americans in a White Man's Land, 1619-2000*, by Francis D. Adams and Barry Sanders.

Once Jesus was asked, "Teacher, which commandment is the greatest in the Law?"

37Jesus declared, "Love the Lord your God with all your heart and with all your soul and with all your mind. 38This is the first and greatest commandment. 39And the second is like it:

'Love your neighbor as yourself.' 40All the Law and the Prophets hang on these two commandments."

If the second one is like the first, love your neighbor with all your heart, your soul, and mind, this means one who claims faith in God and does not love in this way has missed the point.

Beyond religion, as blood flows to sustain life, true love is the life blood of humanity. The message of True Love must circulate.

Love must spread to the hearts and minds of all humanity to extend healthy life. It's up to you to embrace it and live it. By teaching the meaning, you will cause a cognitive reframing in the lives of those you touch.

Lesson 13: The Most Important Thing.

Love is the most important thing in humankind. Not money, airplanes, cars, houses or investments. These things serve us behind love, not in front of it. Keep the Most Important Thing the Most Important Thing.

Exercise:

Create a journal in the back of this book. In it, list ways (in categories) of how you can consistently live in the most powerful force on earth, love, for yourself and others.

Suggested categories:

- For myself
- For my partner
- For children
- For extended family
- For my parents
- For people I pass on the street
- For co-workers
- For employees and contractors
- To help make a more loving world
- For teachers
- For care service providers
- For service workers and co-workers
- For other drivers on the road around me
- For people who are not like me
- For people who don't believe like I believe

There is space available for you to add your own subject in the heading of each page in the journal.

Chapter 14
Love Is the Priority

Without true love in first place, humankind will destroy itself. Please stay optimistic. I spoke some of these truths in Episode 6 - Coronavirus Aftermath Prevention Task force. The truth is there is going to be an Aftermath.

People are going to be without food and shelter as we move forward. People without food and shelter resort to efforts to feed and shelter themselves. This could mean mass rioting and looting unless they receive the help they need.

In an NPR interview, on March 27, 2020, the *Atlantic Magazine* writer expressed that "there will be long term mental effects of the coronavirus."

There will also be financial effects. One thing he said that still rings in my ears today is that,

"The world is vulnerable because of globalization. The only way to solve that is going to be to cooperate with each other."

I believe that cooperation in ways that raise funds, support non-profits and open opportunities are ways to solve the problems that could very well be on the way.

I have a feeling that many people feel the same way I feel. That's why I created the facebook group, *Your Case for Love - My Soulmate Discovery*. It's where we talk about love and how we can get creative sharing it. Should we fundraise to help non-profits help people? Should we practice media preparedness so we can give power filled interviews? It's up for discussion. I invite you to come in and join the discussion.

https://www.facebook.com/groups/yourcaseforlove

My mother was highly empathetic. She served as a missionary leading over 150 non-profit organizations in helping their communities. My brother called me September 15th, 2015 to let me know mom had passed to the other side. The guitar in the background of True Love on the podcast is me playing as the tears streamed down my face. Since that day and much before, Liz has been someone I trust and give my heart.

Before mom left, she was sure to remind me that Love is a commitment. She said,

"Never stop the work of your calling and keep believing in the good in people."

Liz and I agree that, as we develop we will develop a way to be a help to more people.

Join us in helping to spread True Love to humanity, those who need it and who'll welcome it. I invite you right now, to walk with me in keeping love the most important thing.

Volunteers: *They just have the heart to make a difference*

Lesson 14: Cooperate to Support People

Currency distributed as personal, or communal. The government has created ease for communal dollars by enacting tax write offs.

The heart has made it rewarding to help another beyond taxes. Not many would write off giving $2 or $20 to the guy on the corner needing food for his dog or children. Instead, you may ask yourself, "What if it were me in need?"

Exercise:

Create a list of needs and organizations you have a heart to help on the needs and organizations page.

Talk with us or them about your desire to help.
https://www.yourcaseforlove.com/
coronavirustaskforce

Needs:	Organizations:

Liz through the ages

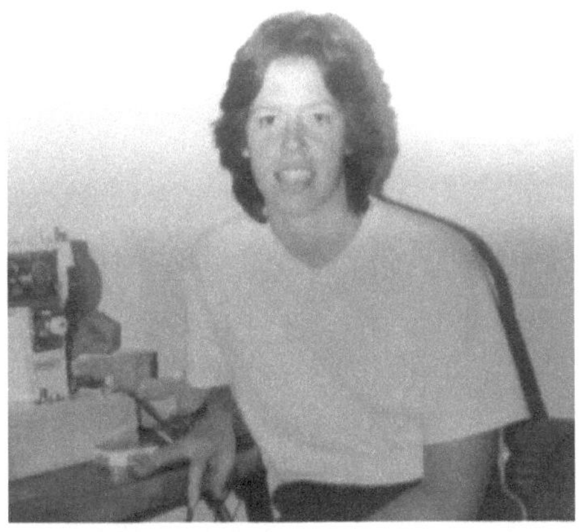

Cherokee Park walking areas

Conclusion

- This personal development guide is now transformed into your reference book.

- Keep the book where you can get to it with ideas for your journal

- Refer to your journal each day until you have your commitments memorized

- Now that you've Finished this book, you've just began to live knowingly in your highest power.

- Be an advocate and show others true love

- Join the facebook group

https://www.facebook.com/groups/yourcaseforlove

Our best to you! Tony and Liz 2010

Sources and Resources

https://en.wikipedia.org/wiki/Bypass_(road)...............page 4

Your Case for Love Podcast

https://www.yourcaseforlove.com/podcasts....................page

12 www.google.com/maps/@goshen.indiana...................page

13 Definition of **lust**...page

17 Photo by Fredrick Eankels from Pexels.........................page

19 https://www.pexels.com/phot o/box-cheerful-color-

cute-207983/...page 22

h t t p s : / / w w w . g o o g l e . c o m / m a p s /

@2124CherokeeParkway ....pages 24 and 25

Route 66 through our 11 hour drive through the Navajo

Nation, Arizona, by Tony Dee.................................page 30

Saint Charles Lewis & Clark exhibit pictures by Tony Dee

....page 32

Saint Charles Settlement pictures by Tony Dee..........page 33

https://www.yourcaseforlove.com/about-tony-dee.page 38

https://www.facebook.com/groups/

yourcaseforlove..page 39

Cherokee Park

https://www.flickr.com/photos/louisvillemetro/albums/

72157627201228504/with/5940527252/

https://www.mindtime.com/ ………………………………………

(please see *The Right Person Challenge*…………………………………

https://www.yourcaseforlove.com/RightPersonChallenge)

Liz and Tony pictures by www.rachelmoorephoto.com

Habit birth: https://quoteinvestigator.com/2013/01/10/

watch-your-thoughts/ **page 65**

My List
Qualities in my partner

Journal

Suggested category For myself or

____

____

____

____

____

____

____

____

____

____

____

____

____

Journal

For my partner or

____

____

____

____

____

____

____

____

____

____

____

____

____

____

Journal

Suggested category

For children or

Journal

Suggested category

For extended family or

____

____

____

____

____

____

____

____

____

____

____

____

Journal

Suggested category

For my parents or

____

____

____

____

____

____

____

____

____

____

____

____

____

Journal

Suggested category

For people I pass on the street or

Journal

Suggested category

For co-workers or

____

____

____

____

____

____

____

____

____

____

____

____

____

Journal

Suggested category

For employees and contractors or

Journal

Suggested category

To help create a loving world or

Journal

Suggested category

For teachers or

Journal

Suggested category

For care providers or

____

Journal

Suggested category

For service workers or

Journal

Suggested category

For drivers on the road or

Journal

Suggested category

For people who aren't like me or

Journal

Suggested category

People who believe different or

Journal

For

Journal

For

Journal

For

Journal

For

Journal

For

Journal

For

Journal

For

Journal

For

Journal

For

Journal

For

Journal

Expectations Conversations Points

Journal

Expectations Conversations Points

Journal

For

Journal

For

Journal

For

Journal

For

Journal

For

Journal

For

____

____

____

____

____

____

____

____

____

____

____

____

____

____

Journal

For

Journal

For

Journal

For

Journal

For

Journal

For

Journal

For

Journal

For

About me, the author

First, congratulations on getting your copy of *Your Case for Love*. A little about me: I've been a happily married introvert for nearly 13 years. *I always felt there was something wonderful about the numbers twelve plus one!* We have seven children total, one in a debilitating condition, three frontline workers, an emergency technician, one an HR manager, and my oldest, a PhD, who I'll share a bit about here.

During our weekly three-hour drives to and from her college dorm, I thought it was a good idea to express to my daughter *What True Love Is* and *How to get a good man*. Both lessons were explained in this book, except for this very one crucial rule: *Get to know men as friends first. No kissing or beyond, no staying over past 8:00pm. No claiming anyone for six months to five years after meeting them. That will give you time to get to know who they really are.*

This way, potential 'use you' friends will drop off. The one remaining will be there because he really cares about you and wants to take good care of you. It should go both ways. You should really care about him and want to take good care of him.

She did it. As a result, she married the best person she could have met. Years later, after many failed relationships, I decided that's what I wanted for myself. This was years before I met my wife.

I had gone back to college long after my art school and music college days. My daughter and I were in college at the same time. This time I'd taken a big bite, attending literary, engineering and business schools at the same time.

I was determined to graduate. Right before graduation my bike brakes locked, I went flying over it, my face smashed into the pavement. The doctors replanted my teeth, wired my jaw, sewed my lip and nose back on and wrapped my broken arm in a cast. They said I was healing too fast. They took the cast off two weeks early, which allowed me to continue my studies without the restraint. The accident happened in October of 2007. I graduated all three schools in December of 2007.

I thoroughly enjoyed taking my daughter to and from school, our talks and me teaching her the power of true love. The problem was, yes, I taught her, but I'd never put my own concepts and understandings to work for myself. Like most people, I had allowed myself to select by emotions. After entering each relationship, I'd scold myself, knowing I went about it all wrong.

It was only after I'd made up my mind to live by what I knew as a best practice for discovering someone who I really fit with, to stop making choices by what I felt. I decided enough was enough. I made up my mind to limit my search for my soul mate by what I know is important to me, not just some excitement I felt.

I'd toured the region singing and playing music with a band. I'd taught school, went to seminary and dug deep into the theological dictionary and other sources, learning the depths of love from many sources and cultures. Then it occurred to me that the love the general public speaks about is a byproduct of romanticism presented by a 17th century leader. It wasn't meant to be described like that, but people have latched on to it because of her importance.

Sex and romance have been substituted with the word love and simply passed on through generations. Knowing that, I decided it's time to be bold, it's time the truth be told. I've studied the subject for over 46 years, to say the least. I've been able to truly live it out in the past 12. I wrote this book to share my discoveries with you.

These are just 14 things you can do. There are many more. Applying these 14 as a foundation will set you well on your way to a *happily ever after* relationship, in each category.

In this time of world change, Liz and I hope this book has taken you on a journey that allowed you the pleasure of knowing True Love and how you can put it into practice in your own life.

Tony Dee, Bachelor in the Science of Business, Certified Neurological Linguistics Practitioner in life changing behavior, Avid Certified Recording Engineer, Graduate in the study of writing children's literature, Founder of the Your Case for Love ByPass Coaching Method and The Education through Music Program.

Please share your Y.C.F.L. discovery

https://www.yourcaseforlove.com

Contact

Get your "COVID-19" Identifier System here:

https://www.yourcaseforlove.com/covid-19-check-sheet

If you purchased from my site, you'll also receive an email
that will contain the opportunity to download the edited
Life Partner Plan template
To build your case for love after you opt-in here.

https://www.yourcaseforlove.com/life-plan-template

Take the Right Person Challenge
https://www.yourcaseforlove.com/the-right-person-challenge

Get my coaching

or

Become a student

https://www.yourcaseforlove.com/the-bypass-method

If you feel you'd like more direct support and accountability
for finding your Right Person, you will benefit from The
ByPass Method One-on-One Coaching. Enter this link and
complete the application:

https://www.yourcaseforlove.com/ByPass-Method-Coaching

or attend the next webinar, where you'll learn just how to
discover your most wonderful right person!

YOUR CASE FOR LOVE